DEALERSHIP DECEIT
How to Buy Your Next Car for Way Less than You can Imagine

Dan Christian

© 2015 DAN CHRISTIAN
dan@dealershipdeceit.com
www.dealershipdeceit.com

ALL RIGHTS RESERVED. NO PART OF THIS WORK MAY BE REPRODUCED OR STORED IN AN INFORMATIONAL RETRIEVAL SYSTEM, WITHOUT THE EXPRESS PERMISSION OF THE PUBLISHER IN WRITING.

ISBN: 9780994771506

PUBLISHED BY:
10-10-10 PUBLISHING
MARKHAM, ON
CANADA

Contents

Foreword	v
Introduction: Your Next Car	1
Chapter 1: New or Used?	11
Chapter 2: Before Entering the Dealership	19
Chapter 3: The Dealership Experience	29
Chapter 4: The "Friendly" Salesperson	35
Chapter 5: The Foursquare of Deception	43
Chapter 6: Leasing	53
Chapter 7: The 2-Dealership Method™	57
Chapter 8: Finance and Insurance	61
Chapter 9: No-Haggle Dealerships	71
Chapter 10: Your Action Plan	75

Foreword

Dealership Deceit by Dan Christian is intended to help you save a great deal of cash on your next dealership purchase. Purchasing a car at a dealership is very daunting and it is very easy to fall into the traps that lead you to paying a higher price than you need to, allowing dealerships to make a tidy profit from novice car buyers – a lot of times without you even knowing it!

Dan has met many people who have purchased their vehicles at dealerships. Many of them only visit one dealership, not even knowing what car they want. They visit the dealership, get approached by a salesperson and ask the salesperson what car they should get. They proceed to test drive the car the salesperson recommends, and then buy the car they test drove right on the spot! They wrongfully believed that they were being offered an excellent price. Had they implemented some of the techniques discussed in *Dealership Deceit* they could have saved thousands on their purchase.

In *Dealership Deceit* you will discover:

- How to ensure you ARE getting the best possible price that the dealership can offer you!
- The 6 things you MUST do even before setting foot in a dealership to ensure you're buying your next car for the best possible price.
- How dealerships upsell and extort tons of extra profit from you without you even noticing.

Dan Christian

- How to get dealerships to voluntarily offer you better and better prices…and much, much more.

You may only buy a car once every 3 to 7 years, but the salespeople at dealerships typically sell 15-30 cars a month. This unfortunately means that they are much more experienced at getting you to pay a higher price than you are at negotiating a lower price. Dealership Deceit will not be able to give you the required negotiating experience; however, it will show you how you can have salespeople at competing dealerships negotiate against each other to ensure you get the best deal!

Raymond Aaron
NY Times Top Ten Best-Selling Author
www.aaron.com

Introduction
Your Next Car

You are likely reading this book because either you or someone you know is looking to purchase a car at a dealership. You also want to ensure that you get the best price and perks possible at the dealership. Well, congratulations! Just by starting to read this book, you are taking the first step toward saving thousands of dollars on your next vehicle purchase! I highly recommend that you take the time to read this entire book and learn everything you can learn about how to negotiate the cost of the car that you're looking to purchase, down to the lowest amount possible. You may be tempted to only skim through this book, or you may just read the bullets at the end of each chapter. I suggest that you read this book from the very beginning to the very end. This way, you'll get the maximum possible benefit. There are a lot of techniques covered in this book; however, I will warn you that not every technique will work 100% of the time. I recommend, though, that you try to implement as much as you can, because if you do everything I recommend in this book, you will end up saving a ton of money, and you may be surprised just how much you will be able to get the dealership to lower their asking price.

How this book will help you

In this book, I'll help you negotiate the price of the car, down to the lowest price possible, and I'll also suggest other ways that you can enjoy the car you desire without having to either purchase it or lease it. It is important to note that this book will discuss how to get the best price possible at a dealership that allows haggling. If you decide to do business at a dealership that does not allow haggling, very few of the techniques related to negotiating on the showroom floor will work, as the value of the trade-in, the purchase price, and the financing that you can get the dealership is set in stone. However, the discussion related to what happens in the finance and insurance office will still be very relevant.

Does this only work for cars?

Throughout this book, I will be discussing how to purchase your next car for way less than you can imagine. However, these techniques will also work if you are purchasing an SUV, truck, motorcycle, etc.. So, when I refer to the purchase of your next car, I am really referring to the purchase of your next car, SUV, truck, motorcycle, minivan, etc., **as long as it's at a car dealership.**

How often do you buy a car?

Well, the better question might actually be: how often do salespeople at dealerships sell cars? A typical person will buy or lease a new or used car every 3 to 7 years. The average salesperson at a dealership will probably sell anywhere from 15 to 30 cars a month. As you can probably guess, if you negotiate one-on-one with the salesperson, the salesperson will have the upper hand on you with regards to experience. Luckily for you, you are reading this book. This book will show you not only how to get back on even terms at the negotiating table; it will show you how to get salespeople at different dealerships to negotiate against each other to give you the best price and incentives possible!

Dealership Deceit

Format

Each chapter, except for the first chapter, will be about the buying process, whether it is what you should know before you enter the dealership, things you should know about once you're in the dealership, or very major steps you need to take during the actual negotiation. At the end of each chapter, there will be a takeaways section where I will summarize the key points and lessons within each chapter in bullet point form.

Free bonuses at www.dealershipdeceit.com

I also have many free bonuses at www.dealershipdeceit.com. Be sure to check these out! Free bonuses that you will get at this website include: a glossary which explains the meanings of some of the technical terms and dealership jargon mentioned throughout this book, a spreadsheet you can use to calculate the monthly payment and lease payments you should be making, a printable version of the action plan at the end of this book, and a story about my most recent dealership purchase, where I learnt most of the techniques mentioned throughout this book. You will also find a listing of useful websites where you can check out the wholesale and dealer invoice prices of vehicles. I don't mention these websites in this book because web addresses and website information change on a regular basis and I want you to have the most up-to-date information possible.

Some key points will be mentioned more than once

Some techniques and key points will be mentioned more than once throughout this book, as some of these techniques may be relevant to more than one aspect of the negotiation and car buying process. Again, I urge you to read everything in this book from the very beginning to the very end, and I urge you to implement and utilize as much of the techniques and strategies as you can so you can get the most benefit from this book, and ultimately pay as little as possible for your vehicle.

The mindset

At the time of writing this book, most dealerships require that you haggle with them to ensure that they do not make a hefty profit at your expense. There are a few dealerships where the price shown on their website or listed on the car itself, i.e. the sticker price, is the actual price that you will be paying for the vehicle. These are no-haggle dealerships. If the salesperson or the dealership manager at these dealerships allows you to haggle with them, their image and reputation will be tarnished. Their brand would be in jeopardy. If the thought of having to haggle with the dealership really scares you, purchasing your car at a no-haggle dealership may be very attractive. However, please note that just because you are buying your car at a no-haggle dealership doesn't mean that the dealership will not try to extort extra profit from you, nor will you not be able to find a better deal at a dealership that requires haggling.

Whether or not you decide to buy your car at a no-haggle dealership or at a dealership where you have to haggle, you will need to get into the right mindset. This means that you will have to be very knowledgeable about what the absolute minimum amount is that you can purchase your car for, and if your car is a new car, what incentives the manufacturer is offering that month. This also means that you will need to employ the Law of Attraction to ensure you focus on getting the price you desire for both your trade-in and the vehicle you're looking to purchase.

The Law of Attraction

When you employ the Law of Attraction, you program your conscious and subconscious mind to enable you to do what you need to do in order to get the price you desire. If you can convince yourself that you will purchase your car at a certain price, and that price is reasonable, you will subconsciously do what's necessary to get your car for that particular price. If you believe you won't be able to negotiate down your car to your target price point, it will become impossible for you. If you believe you can negotiate down your car down to your target price point, and not only that but believe it's the price you deserve to pay for that car, you will get the car for that price. What is your target price point? You need to believe that you can buy your car for the dealer cost, i.e. dealer invoice cost, in the case of a new car, and wholesale in the case of a used car. If you plan to sell your current car to the dealership, i.e. trade it in, you also need to believe you can sell your car to the dealership for at least its current wholesale value. You can visit www.dealershipdeceit.com to approximate the dealer invoice price for new cars, and the wholesale price for used cars.

Getting back to the Law of Attraction, for example, if you can, and believe that you should, purchase your next car for only $20,000, you will subconsciously program your brain to do what is necessary to find a way to purchase the car for only $20,000. If you believe that $20,000 is impossible for you to attain, and you believe that the best price you can actually get it for is $22,000, you will inevitably end up paying $22,000 for your car. Of course, the price must be reasonable. Even if you want to buy your car for only $50, no dealership will sell you a car for $50.

Buying from a car dealership is a very emotionally draining process; you will need to stay sharp and focused throughout the entire process. Be warned, if you use the tips discussed in this book, the salesperson, the dealership manager, and the finance and insurance manager at the dealership that you will be visiting will become very agitated and frustrated dealing with you. You need to have thick skin when you're implementing these strategies. You will have to be at peace with knowing that some people in several dealerships will be aggravated if you want to get the best price possible. If the thought of intentionally annoying people doesn't sit well with you, you may want to consider bringing along a friend or family member with you when you negotiate at the various dealerships. Dealerships that are trying to sell you a car will count on the fact that you are afraid of annoying the staff. They use this fear to deceive and coerce you into paying a higher price than you should. This means more profit for the dealership.

This book will also ask that you leave a deposit at more than one dealership, and at some point you will need to have all but one of these deposits returned to you. Asking for a deposit to be returned is a very arduous process. Salespeople and managers are trained to hard sell you a car when you enter a dealership. They'll try even harder to close you once you leave a deposit with them. Leaving a deposit with a dealership is essentially showing the dealership that you are a motivated buyer. They'll do everything they can to make you close a deal, and they will make you feel very guilty about attempting to get your deposit back. You have to be willing to fight hard enough to get your deposits back from all the dealerships (except for the dealership you will eventually buy your car from, though the fighting is not over, even with this dealership).

Of course, try not to be a jerk when you use these methods. Try to be as positive as possible, or at least understanding that you're going to end up making more than one dealership work hard for your sale, which will earn them less profit and commission than from a typical car buyer.

Timing

A common question is: when should I buy my car? Or better stated, what is the best time of month or year to buy my car? Well, dealerships usually set sales targets for their salespeople in three categories: monthly goals, quarterly goals, and annual goals. So, you likely have a better chance of getting a lower price for your car if you buy near the end of the month, and at the end of each fiscal quarter i.e. March, June, September, and December. If the dealership represents a manufacturer that is publically traded, i.e. Dodge or Honda or Volkswagen, you will probably have the best chance of getting your car at the best price at the end of the financial fiscal year, i.e. March. Dealerships that represent publicly traded manufacturers need to report to their shareholders every quarter. If sales are lagging, they will very likely do what they can to increase the number of cars being sold and make their financial situation look better in the eyes of their shareholders, i.e. incentivize dealerships to sell tons of cars.

Also, I would consider looking at June, especially if you're looking to purchase a brand-new car. Not only is June the end of a quarter, but it is also when manufacturers start selling next year's models. If your intent is purchasing a brand-new car, I suggest waiting until right before next year's model comes out, as the dealership will likely be discounting the current year's model in an effort to try to get them off their lot as soon as possible. You will still get a brand-new car, it's just your car will be a lot cheaper than if you try purchasing it earlier during the year. If you intend to lease a new car, I would actually avoid initiating a lease agreement in June as the value of your car might dramatically fall right when the new models are released, and this may affect the value of your car at the end of the lease, which will increase your monthly depreciation payments. More this will be discussed later in the leasing chapter.

Takeaways

- Read the entire book! And do everything this book tells you to do (or as much as you can possibly can).

- Before you enter the dealership, you will need to be willing to get the right mindset. This means you should employ the law of attraction and believe that you can get the dealership to sell you the car for your target price. This also means that you will need to develop a thick skin when negotiating with salespeople and managers. More often than not you will be annoying and frustrating them, and if the thought of intentionally annoying others is against your nature, please bring a friend or family member to help you with the negotiation.

- Look to buy your car at either the end of the month, at the end of the fiscal quarter, or at the end of the fiscal year. Also, if you're looking to buy a new car, consider looking at the end of June. June is the time when manufacturers roll out their next year's models, and dealerships are likely trying to get rid of their year old models. But, don't initiate a new lease in June.

Be sure to check out the free bonuses at www.dealershipdeceit.com!

Dealership Deceit

Summary

This chapter should give you some insight as to what to expect in this book, and also shed some light into the car buying process. The next chapter will help you decide whether you should purchase a new or used car, and will help you determine if you should purchase or lease your next car.

Chapter 1
New or Used?

The intent of this book is to help you save as much money as possible on your next dealership purchase. Whether or not you follow this advice is totally up to you. In this chapter I'm going to highly recommend against purchasing a new car in any situation. This is because the market value of a new car drops dramatically the second it is driven off a lot. However, please feel free to purchase whichever car you would like to purchase. Just know that if you purchase a new car, the value of your car will drop quickly, after you complete the purchase.

You should evaluate your own needs carefully and make a decision for yourself as to what kind of car you want to purchase. Narrowing down exactly what model of car you should buy is outside of the scope of this book. You may just want a car to commute from home to work, or you may want a top-of-the-line sports car to help you show off to your friends and family. You may need a minivan to transport your family between soccer and dance practices, or you might need a pickup truck if you are a contractor. If you are a real estate agent, you may need to be driving a top-of-the-line BMW or Mercedes or even a Tesla. If you just need a car to get back and forth from work and home, you may be able to get away with a used compact car or a midsized car. Horsepower may be your biggest concern, or fuel economy, or safety. No matter what type of car you need to purchase, going the right route with regards to whether you should buy new or used, or purchase or lease, will save you thousands of dollars.

Do I even need to purchase another car?

First of all, you should narrow down why you want to purchase another car. If your family is starting to grow, and you currently own a coupe, purchasing a larger car such as an SUV or a minivan makes perfect sense. If you have a regular midsized car but you plan to take a job as a realtor selling high-end luxury homes, leasing a top-of-the-line high-end luxury car makes sense. If your car is 20 years old and on its last legs, it makes sense for you to purchase a newer car. Likely, it'll be cheaper for you to purchase another car than to fix your current car.

If you just want a new car because you're getting bored of your current car, and your current car is less than 10 years old, maybe another option for you to consider is to improve your current car. For instance, you can consider getting your car detailed. I recently had my car detailed at a specialty carwash, and when the car was returned to me, I did not even recognize it. I felt like I purchased a new car! The car was very clean inside, and it even smelled like a new car. The best part was that I only paid $200 for the service. A new car or even another used car would've cost me way more than the $200 that I spent at the car wash. Other things you can do are install a new sound system or a new radio. You could even have satellite radio installed on your current car, or an updated alarm system which links to your phone. Of course this is going to cost you money, but it will cost much less than it would for you to purchase another car at a dealership.

If you want to purchase a new car because the car you're looking to purchase just came out with a brand new feature that you're in love with, I would either suggest leasing the car or waiting a couple years if possible and then purchasing that particular model as a used car.

The case of a new fancy sports car or new luxury car

In my opinion, the only financially beneficial reason for you to be in possession of a top-of-the-line BMW or Mercedes, or even a Lamborghini or Ferrari, is that you need to show your clients that you are wealthy (unless you're renting one for a weekend or two for the fun of it). Naturally, as you may know, people associate your level of wealth with the car you drive. If people see you driving around in a top-of-the-line BMW, they will naturally assume that you're wealthy (even if you're not). However, it is very natural for anyone, wealthy or not, to want to own one of these high-end cars.

If you are a wealthy businessperson, and you need a top-of-the-line car to show your clients that you are indeed wealthy, consider leasing your high-end car. When you lease a car from the dealership, you are essentially renting the car, and your monthly rent payment will be the depreciation of the car plus an interest rate, as well any other fees and taxes the dealership or manufacturer may tag on. The depreciation curve of a new car is very steep compared to that of a used car. New cars on average lose 20 to 30% of their value the second you drive them off the lot, and although the curve eases up after a couple of years, almost all cars will continue to depreciate over time.

If you need a top-of-the-line car to impress your clients on a regular basis, you will likely need to trade it in after three or four years for a newer version of the top-of-the-line model. When the time comes for you to trade that vehicle in, you will be shocked as to its true value. The rule of any investment (not just a vehicle) is purchase what appreciates in value and rent what depreciates in value. A properly negotiated lease contract will only require you to pay for the depreciation of the car plus interest, with minimal profit for the dealership. More of this will be discussed in the leasing chapter, but when you lease a car you essentially pay the difference between the purchase price if you were to purchase the car and a best guess at the market value of the car at the end of the lease.

If you are not wealthy but you still desire to drive a top-of-the-line new car, it would be better for you to rent that particular car for a weekend or a couple of weekends every so often. You likely do not need to experience the thrill of driving a very fancy sports car every day. If you want that car to show off to somebody, just rent the car when you need to. They likely won't know you're just renting it for the weekend. They will just see you in a high-end Mercedes and they will be thoroughly impressed. If you need a high-end car to impress someone you're dating, trying to spend money you cannot afford to spend to make unaffordable payments for a rapidly depreciating asset will not make you look good in the long term as you likely will not have money for anything else. Also, if somebody only likes you because you driving a very expensive car, I don't know if this is the person you want to have a long-term relationship with.

For every other situation, from a financial standpoint I suggest buying a used car over a new car. Actually, I never suggest buying a new car. Buying a used car makes more sense than buying a new car because used cars depreciate much more slowly than new cars, as shown in the following figure. Also, used cars are much cheaper than new cars, so it will be easier for you to pay off a loan on a used car than a new car.

If you take a look at the following figure showing the value of an average new $25,000 car, you will notice that it drops in value by $7,500 in the first year and another $2,500 in the second year. The yearly drop in value becomes less and less dramatic as we get to year three and beyond.

Dealership Deceit

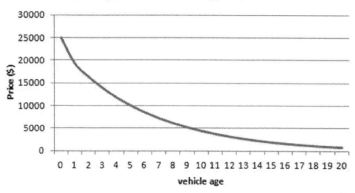

Credit: retireby40.org

You may be interested to know that dealerships make significantly more money on the showroom floor from a used car than they do from a new car. When a typical car buyer purchases their next new or used car, they usually come in knowing what the dealer invoice or wholesale price is of the car they're looking to buy. For some reason, car buyers significantly underestimate the value of their trade-in. Car buyers do not usually have an issue trading in their car for $2,500 when in reality the car is worth $6,000. If the dealership can fix the $6,000 car for $1,000 and sell it for $8,000, they will have made a **$4,500** profit on a $2,500 purchase. Manufacturers make all their money on new cars, so it is imperative to them that dealerships keep buying new cars from them on a regular basis.

If you are concerned with the value of your car depreciating as slowly as possible, I would suggest picking a Japanese car over an American or German car. Japanese cars tend to retain their value more easily than American or German cars over time. The repair costs for Japanese cars also tend to be lower than that of German cars.

My last suggestion for this chapter is if you worried about keeping your repair costs as low as possible, purchase a very popular model. An example of a popular model is a Toyota Corolla or a Honda Civic. Finding parts for these cars tends to be very easy, and these types of cars are easy for mechanics to service (as opposed to, say, a BMW X6). Therefore, repair costs for these types of vehicles are lower than for less popular models or for German models.

Takeaways

- If your desire for another car stems out of desire rather than need, first consider improving your current car. Improving your current car could turn out to be a lot cheaper than purchasing or leasing a new or used car.

- From a financial point of view, always consider purchasing a used car, not a new car.

- If you are wealthy and you need a top-of-the-line new car to show your clients that you are wealthy, lease. Top-of-the-line cars depreciate very quickly, and leasing and getting a new lease when your current lease is up may be more financially beneficial than purchasing your new top-of-the-line car.

- If you are not wealthy, but you still want a top-of-the-line car to show off, consider renting the car of your dreams for a weekend every couple months or so.

- If you don't know which model to pick, and you want your car to depreciate as slowly as possible and your servicing costs to be as low as possible, consider a popular Japanese model.

Dealership Deceit

Be sure to check out the free bonuses at www.dealershipdeceit.com!

Hopefully this chapter helped you decide whether you want to purchase or lease your next new or used vehicle. In the next chapter, I will show you what kind of research you need to do and what you need to know before you enter your first dealership. The information contained in the next chapter is very important, as it will prevent you from getting overcharged at the dealership.

Chapter 2
Before Entering the Dealership

This chapter will tell you about six things that you must absolutely know and do before you enter a dealership. In order to get the most benefit out of this book, and to ensure you get the best deal possible, it is very highly recommended that you read and practice all six concepts listed in this chapter. However, the rest of this book will be written as if you've done nothing in this chapter and skipped over it. Please note that if you do not do one or more of these things listed in this chapter, you will likely not save as much money as you could have, and this will mean more profit for the dealership from your purchase.

If you're planning to do a trade in, sell your car privately beforehand

If you're planning to trade your car in at the dealership, consider selling it privately first. It is very convenient to trade your car into the dealership; however, dealerships tend to pay you way less than your car is worth, and then turn around and sell your car for way more than it's worth.

There are techniques that the salesperson and the dealership manager will use to deceive you into thinking your car is not worth as much as you personally think it is. Paying you significantly less for your car, then turning it around and selling it for much more than it's worth is a major source of revenue for the dealership, and doing this will land the salesperson a large commission.

Although you will be selling your car privately (hopefully!), it is best that you do not tell the salesperson at the dealership that you're doing so, at least not right away. If the salesperson thinks you're planning to trade your car in at the dealership, the salesperson and the dealership manager will likely be open to selling you the car for a lower price because they're anticipating making a ton of profit from the car you're trading in.

As mentioned earlier, salespeople and dealership managers have techniques to deceive you into thinking your car is not worth as much as you think it is. At some point, either the salesperson or the dealership manager will walk around and drive the vehicle that you plan to sell them. One technique they'll use is when they walk around your vehicle, they will point to very minor imperfections such as paint chips and very minor dents, but they won't say anything out loud. They might also ask you very odd questions where the answer is very obvious from looking at your car, like if your car has air-conditioning or four-wheel-drive or heated seats when it obviously does not.

This is all psychological manipulation. They are trying to make you think that your car is not worth as much as it actually is. To find out how much your car is actually worth visit the websites listed at www.dealershipdeceit.com. There is a very low chance, though, that the dealership will give you the actual value of your car as a credit towards the purchase of your next car unless they overinflate the purchase price or massively overinflate your financing costs (should you choose to finance at the dealership). You will very likely get a better purchase price if you sell your car on Craigslist or Kijiji, or to your friends. If you want to get paid the most for your trade-in, sell it privately. Don't sell it to the dealership.

Get your financing sorted beforehand

Get your financing sorted out before you enter the dealership. Approach banks and credit unions and possibly even brokers to find out what you can afford, how much they can lend you for your next car, and what kind of interest rate you qualify for. Also find out how much you can put down or you need to put down to get your next car. As will be explained later, dealerships love to play a game with you where they find out how much of a monthly payment you're willing to pay, and then trick you or deceive you into paying a higher interest rate than you would need to pay if you financed through a bank or a credit union. Dealerships may trick you into paying as much as a 10 or 11% interest rate just by convincing you to pay an extra $50 or even $100 per month more then you originally intended to. If you do not personally go to your bank yourself and you do not figure out what kind of percent interest rate you qualify for, you will not know if you can qualify for something as low as 3% or if you can only qualify for something as high as 11%. If you plan to finance through the dealership, the dealership will just approach your bank (or another similar bank) and find out what interest rate you actually qualify for, then they'll write you a contract telling you to pay a bit more than the interest rate you actually qualify for.

Say you easily qualify for a 5% interest rate but you don't know this because you're financing through the dealership and you didn't think to approach your bank and ask. The dealership knows you qualify for 5%. So, in the interest of making as much profit as possible, the dealership tells you that the lowest interest rate you qualify for is 10% because there are some issues with your credit (they like to pull your credit information while you take your test drive). They will also make up some story about how the bank originally rejected your application, but they were able to tell the bank how nice and trustworthy you are, and they (the dealership) were able to do you a favor. They are trying to make the bank look like bad guys and themselves look like the hero. Without the dealership, you would have not been able to qualify for a loan and you would not have been able to purchase the car. The dealership has a copy of your credit report, so they can see what loans and credit cards you have, and they are not afraid to make up stories to convince you your credit is not as good as it actually is. So, feeling very grateful towards the dealership, you sign a contract where you end up paying a 10% interest rate. The bank lending the money is only getting 5%. Where does the extra 5% go? Pure profit for the dealership.

Go to your bank, and figure out what you can be preapproved for. Don't let the dealership artificially inflate your interest rate and make themselves out to be the hero.

Just like the previous tip, it may be advantageous to not let the dealership know early on that you have financed previously, until you negotiate a purchase price. The dealership may be willing to give you a better purchase price if they think they can make a hefty profit on your financing.

Know your budgeted down payment and monthly payment

Are you ready to buy a car? Are you upside down (i.e. you owe more on your current car than you can sell for)? You may have the urge to buy a newer car, but can you really afford to do so? How to determine how much you can afford to pay for your next car based on your current income and expenditures is outside of the scope of this book; however, you should know how much you can afford. Knowing how much you can afford for a monthly car payment and what interest rate you qualify

Dealership Deceit

for should help you figure the maximum allowable purchase price for your next car. This will be discussed later, but you should always primarily negotiate the purchase price. If you're really set on financing through the dealership, you need to know what your maximum allowable monthly payment is, based on your personal budget, and you need to stick to it! Know what your maximum monthly payment is, and do not let the dealership go over that number in any way whatsoever. The common tactic during the negotiation process or during the conversation is the "up to" question.

Up to?

The salesperson will ask you what you're looking to pay on a monthly basis. After thinking about how much you can afford for a payment, you will either likely tell the salesperson a number, say $150, or you will likely give the salesperson a range, say $250-$300. The salesperson will then ask you "up to"? Most people subconsciously will add $50 or $100 to the previous number they gave. At that point, the salesperson will proceed to sell you a car at a price point just barely under the upper limit that you gave after answering the up to question. Of course your monthly payment will shoot way past his number once you navigate through the finance and insurance phase, but more on that later. Either way, that extra $50 or $100 will have netted the dealership an extra $3,000-$12,000 profit if you're financing over five or seven years.

Know what your budgeted down payment is, get your financing dealt with separately through a bank or credit union, and if you're financing with the dealership make sure they do not go higher than the monthly payment that you specify. Make sure they don't "up to" you.

23

Know what vehicle you want to purchase and what the actual value is

Helping you decide what kind of car you want to purchase is outside of the scope of this book. One thing I would suggest is look up the consumer ratings of the cars that pique your interest. When you do this, make sure that the ratings you're looking at are rating cars that are manufactured in your country or area (the manufacturer of a Honda Civic in Japan will be different than the one in the US) and make sure you check the ratings of the model and year of the car you're looking at.

Once you decide what kind of car you want to purchase, look around to see which dealerships are selling that car. Often, there'll be more than one dealership with the car that you want. There's a chance that these dealerships may not be in your home town. Each of these dealerships will have a car you want, but the purchase price listed is probably not the price you want to pay. Either way, what you want to do is find the dealerships that have the car you want and then you want to make appointments with them to see the car to make sure that they actually have the car in stock. You may even want to consider putting down a deposit over the phone to ensure that they indeed do have the car on the lot. Sometimes dealerships will post a car on their website for a very attractive price. But, when you visit the dealership and ask to see the car, it very well may be gone or the car is there but the trim level of the actual car is at a lower grade than the trim level listed on the website. Their goal is to get you in the dealership in the first place so they can start hard selling you. Listing cars on their website at lower than expected prices is one way dealerships attract people into their dealership.

To find out the actual value of the car you're looking for, if it's a new car, you'll need to find out the dealer invoice price. The

Dealership Deceit

dealer invoice price is how much the dealership paid for the new car from the manufacturer. If you're purchasing a used car, you will want to find out what the wholesale price or black book price is. The wholesale price or black book price is how much the dealership would typically pay for the car at an auction.

Simply googling the dealer invoice price of a vehicle will certainly give you interesting results. Be careful, though; many websites that claim to give you the actual dealer invoice price for a vehicle actually take your information and forward it on to a dealership who will then contact you in an effort to hard-sell you on that vehicle.

Also, in the case of a new vehicle, you should see what rebates or other incentives the manufacturer has available for your car for that month. The value of these rebates and incentives vary month-to-month, so you should be checking this on a regular basis. You should also know how long and what the manufacturer's warranty is whether you're looking for a new or a used vehicle. When you're looking for a used car, consider purchasing used cars that are still under the manufacturer's warranty. You can probably guess this, but if the car is still under the manufacturer's warranty there is very little value in purchasing an extra extended warranty from the dealership.

Know who regulates dealerships in your state or province

There will likely come a time when the dealership will refuse to do something that you know they ethically and legally have to do. This usually happens when you ask for your deposit back. Dealerships like to make up excuses as to why you suddenly cannot get your refundable deposit back. You will need to threaten to report the dealership, and you're going to need to

25

know who licenses dealerships in your area. Before entering a dealership in your state or province, you need to need to know who this person or agency is. I would suggest doing a search on "who regulates car dealerships in [your state or province]". Very likely this government department will be associated in some way with the Department of Motor Vehicles or DMV if you are in the United States.

Know when during the process you cannot walk away and you have officially bought the car

If you've left a deposit, you'll need to know for yourself when you can still ask for the deposit back or when you have officially bought the car, and not let the dealership tell you otherwise. Salespeople, dealership managers, and finance insurance managers will use all kinds of ways to deceive you into thinking you have officially bought your car. Until you have signed the bottom of the purchase agreement, the dealership has the keys to your trade-in, and you have the keys to the car the dealership is selling you in your hand, you have not bought the car. At any time before this you have the right to walk away, and you have the right to ask for any refundable deposits back. Do not let the dealership coerce you into thinking you have officially bought the car before this point. And if for some "magical" reason your deposit suddenly becomes un-refundable, threaten to go to the dealership's licensing body mentioned in the previous bullet. In the United States, this is likely some branch of the DMV. In Canada, there is a provincial or territorial licensing body which licenses dealerships and allows them to sell cars.

Takeaways

- Sort out as much as you can before entering any dealership, i.e. planning to sell your current car privately and getting

Dealership Deceit

your financing sorted out. You will want to be only negotiating the final purchase price at the dealership.

- Figure out what car you want to buy before entering any dealership, and figure out which dealership has these cars. You will want to know if you want to buy new or used, and you want to know if you intend to lease or purchase outright.

- Know what the dealer invoice price is if you're looking for a new vehicle, and know the wholesale value of your car is if you're looking for a used car.

- You may not get the dealership invoice or wholesale price for the car you're looking to purchase because the dealership needs to make some money off the purchase. But, you will likely be in a better negotiation position if you know what the dealership invoice or the wholesale price is of the car you're looking to purchase.

- Know the length of the manufacturer's warranty, and know if the manufacturer is offering any rebates or any other incentives. Make sure that the dealership does not end up offering you these rebates and incentives as part of the negotiation process, as you are entitled to them whether or not the dealership offers them to you.

Be sure to check out the free bonuses at www.dealershipdeceit.com!

In this chapter, we have discussed six things you need to know before you even enter a dealership. Knowing and doing everything stated in this chapter will give you a massive advantage when negotiating for your next car at a dealership.

Dan Christian

The more you employ the techniques discussed in this book, the better the price you will get at the dealership; of course it is highly recommended that you do everything specified in this chapter. In the next chapter, we will discuss how dealerships are set up to put you at a massive disadvantage and deceive you into paying more than you should.

Chapter 3
The Dealership Experience

Why would people buy cars from dealerships? There are other places to buy cars. You can buy a car at an auction, or you can buy a car from a service such as Craigslist or Kijiji. Well, dealerships have a better selection of vehicles than either Craigslist or Kijiji. Also, you can rest assured that the quality of the vehicle purchased from a dealership (at least a reputable one) is better than at an auction. When you buy a car from an auction, or from Craigslist or Kijiji, there is no guarantee that the car will be in excellent running condition, and there's no guarantee that the maintenance is up to date on the car. When you buy a car from a reputable dealership, even a used car, there is a very good chance that the maintenance on your car will be up to date at the time of purchase, and everything will be in great working condition. Also, dealerships provide one-stop shopping. They are more than happy to buy your old car from you (most of the time for less than it is actually worth), and they will provide financing for you on the spot. Most people love the convenience of being able to sell their car and get financing at the same time, and the same place. Keep in mind, though, there is a very high price for this. Dealerships will almost always buy your car for way less than it is actually worth, and dealerships will always provide you a higher interest rate on any financing than you can easily get on your own.

Most dealerships all around the world are laid out in almost the exact same fashion. There is a big welcoming entrance, there is a showroom inside the entrance where there are a lot of shiny and fancy cars for you to take a look at, touch, and sit inside.

There are offices and/or cubicles either at the back of the showroom or scattered throughout the showroom where customers can negotiate with the salesperson. Next to the showroom, there is usually a service center where customers can have their vehicles serviced. Somewhere in the back hidden behind the showroom, you will find a long hallway with offices. This is usually where the finance and insurance offices are. This is where customers are usually led once a purchase price is agreed to on the showroom floor. You also may notice an office on the showroom floor which is larger in size than the rest of the offices. Usually, this office will have big glass windows, and may even be situated higher than the rest of the offices on the showroom floor. The dealership manager resides here. From here, the dealership manager keeps a watchful eye on the goings-on in the dealership. He or she keeps an eye on all the customers in the showroom, and ensures that each of these customers is being helped by a salesperson. Also, over the course of the negotiation the salespeople will bring numbers that they and the customers agree upon, to the dealership manager for approval.

The Casino

When you drive into the parking lot of a casino, you'll notice a beautiful grand entrance. There is a huge beautiful grand entrance where limos can drop you off or valet drivers take and park your car while you just walk right in. As you enter the casino, you will notice that there are a lot of beautiful lights everywhere. It's very welcoming. The sounds are very intoxicating. This is all to make you feel like you want to start gambling. However, if you take a look anywhere other than at the tables or the machines, you will start to notice peculiar things. The carpet in most casinos is very gaudy. This is because casino owners do not want you to look at it. Also, the ceilings of

Dealership Deceit

most casinos are dark black and bland. Casino owners do not want you looking at the ceiling either. They just want you to focus on the beautiful slot machines and the tables. Actually, you will notice that there are no windows or clocks in a casino. Casino owners want you to get addicted to gambling and lose your sense of time. If there is a clock in the casino or if you can look outside and see that it is getting dark and getting late, you'll start getting the feeling after a while that it is time to leave. This is not what casino owners want. There is even trickery at work at the restaurant in the casino. When you visit the casino restaurant, you will notice that it typically takes a very long time to be seated, even if there's no lineup. There is a reason for this. The casino owner wants you to wait in line for a really long time. They want the line-up to the restaurant to spill over onto the gaming floor. Their thoughts, and they are usually correct about this, are that if a husband and wife wait in line for the buffet or the restaurant, and they end up waiting for a really long time, either the husband or the wife well tell their partner "hey can I just play for a bit while you hold our place in line?" Casinos do not make as much money at the restaurant as they do on the gaming floor. Casinos will go so far as to offer morning and lunch buffets for a very, very reasonable price because they want you to become bored waiting in the seemingly slow line. They are hoping that you get tired, bored, and then start playing one of the machines. The longer you are on the gaming floor, the less time you spend in the restaurant, the more money the casino will make.

Dealerships are not unlike casinos. Dealerships also have a big beautiful façade. The lot and the entranceway are both very welcoming. There is a dealership in my home town that has a beautiful 5 storey glass tower. In this glass tower, there are a couple Lexuses on every storey. You see this tower when you're driving down the state highway from the airport to the city. When you enter a dealership, you will notice that there are lots of beautiful cars everywhere, and you'll even notice that the smell and the atmosphere are very welcoming. That gorgeous new car smell is everywhere! They even have free snacks, free coffee, and free soda or pop for you. The architecture is just so beautiful! There is a really high ceiling and there are enormous windows everywhere. There are all these beautiful cars everywhere that you see when you start walking around the sales floor. Most likely, these will be the most up-to-date models with the highest end trim kits. All this new technology will be very fascinating. You may not notice this at first, but finding the exit once you're in the showroom is a little harder than finding the entrance to the dealership from the parking lot. This is not unlike a casino. Dealerships want you to stay a while; at least long enough for you to buy a car from them.

The prison

Dealerships are not unlike prisons in a sense either. You cannot sneak into a dealership; you either need to sign in with the receptionist, or you will need to be acknowledged by a receptionist or salesperson right at the entrance. When you stroll around the showroom and the lot, you will always be under the careful watch of a salesperson and/or the dealership manager. When prisoners stroll around a prison facility, they are always under the careful watch of a prison guard. If a prisoner wants to leave prison, they will need to get by someone at the front desk. If you want to leave the dealership, you will likely need to get by somebody at the front desk as well. Also, prisons have guard towers where guards stand at the top behind glass windows, watching the movements of the prisoners within and outside of the facility. Dealerships also have similar towers, but dealership towers are manned by dealership managers. These managers keep a watchful eye on all the customers within the dealership, as well as the salespeople. Each customer needs to

Dealership Deceit

be escorted by a salesperson, even at a distance if the customer wishes to be left alone. Dealership managers keeping a watchful eye on their salespeople ensure that each and every customer will be hard sold.

Takeaways

- Dealerships, not unlike casinos, are very purposefully laid out. They are designed to attract people into the dealership, and once in the dealership they are designed to make the customer buy a vehicle rather than leave the dealership.

- Dealerships are also somewhat designed like a prison in the sense that if you want to leave, you will need to get by a person behind a desk, i.e. the prison guard. Also, dealerships and prisons have towers. The dealership tower is manned by the dealership manager, and the prison tower is manned by a prison guard. The dealership manager will keep an eye on the customers, and will direct salespeople to ensure that all customers, even those who are just casually looking at the vehicles, are attended to.

Be sure to check out the free bonuses at www.dealershipdeceit.com!

This chapter gave you some idea as to how dealerships are laid out and set up to emulate casinos and prisons. They may look very welcoming and beautiful, but in actuality they are designed to lure you in and, once you're in, to be hard sold by a salesperson. In the next chapter, we will discuss a bit more about who these salespeople really are, and why they are so desperate to sell you a car.

Chapter 4
The "Friendly" Salesperson

The truth about car salespeople

Being a salesperson at a dealership is a very difficult job. When the barista at a coffee shop asks you if they can help you, you do not feel offended. You either tell the barista your order or that you're still deciding which coffee you want to purchase. When you're greeted by the receptionist at the doctor's office, you do not feel offended. When the receptionist or the nurse at the desk asks you why you came to the doctor's office, you simply answer. You tell them what ailment you have. However, when you enter a dealership and a salesperson approaches you, most people feel offended. People are scared that they will be tricked into buying a car they don't want, for a price that is much higher than they should pay. They are also scared that they will be judged by their peers for being tricked into buying a new car. Or they just genuinely want to be left alone to look at the cars in peace. You will very likely tell the salesperson that you're "just looking" and you will politely (or maybe not so politely) tell the salesperson to leave you alone and that you'll tell him when you need help. The difference here is that at a coffee shop, or at a doctor's office, the livelihood of their job does not rely on whether or not you purchase a coffee or have your ailments treated. At a dealership, the livelihood of the salesperson depends on whether or not you buy a car from them. If the salesperson does not sell a car, she does not eat. A low commission is much better than no commission. This is why salespeople at dealerships are very likely to be way more aggressive than baristas at a coffee shop or receptionists at a doctor's office.

35

Why does that salesperson keep harassing me? I said I am just looking

It is very hard not to notice that as soon as you enter a dealership you will be accosted by a salesperson. Sometimes there are salespeople waiting right outside the dealership entrance. Why is that? Well, it's very natural to assume it's because they want to make as much money as possible, so they hard sell as many people as they can. While this is true in many cases, there is another reason. It's because they're afraid of their manager.

Believe it or not, in many cases salespeople resent their dealership managers. As discussed earlier, the dealership manager in the tower is not unlike the prison guard in the tower. Car salespeople are under just as much scrutiny as the customer. If a salesperson leaves a potential customer alone to look around the dealership without hard selling them on a vehicle, the dealership manager will likely see this and will express their disappointment to the salesperson later on. There are cases where salespeople get sent home for the day or even fired right on the spot, just because they let a customer who told him that they're "just looking" around the dealership actually just look around the dealership. Salesperson turnover rates are, unsurprisingly, very high. There is the potential to earn a lot of money working at a dealership as a salesperson, but you have to be very good at harassing customers and forcing them to buy cars they don't want to buy. Salespeople can be fired and hired in an instant.

How much do salespeople make?

You may also wonder how much money a salesperson makes. Salespeople at dealerships typically make around $250-$500 per sale. Typically a dealership will make $4,000-$10,000 or even

Dealership Deceit

more on the sale of a vehicle (of course not to you because you're reading this book) and salespeople will get 20 to 30% commission. Salespeople are also likely to get a bonus for selling a certain number of cars by a certain deadline. Most often this deadline is the end of the month, fiscal quarter, and fiscal year. This is why it was mentioned earlier that you should purchase at these times; salespeople get bonuses for reaching certain monthly, quarterly, and yearly goals. Also, typical salespeople sell about 15 to 20 cars per month and a good salesperson can sell 25 to 30 cars per month. You can expect a typical car salesperson to make about $60,000-$100,000 per year.

The initial conversation

If you have not completed the homework in Chapter 2, and you're visiting a dealership just to look around, when a salesperson approaches you they will typically start a conversation and ask what you're looking for. After establishing rapport, they will find out how they can help you dump your car and buy one of theirs. This first involves asking you what kind of car you are currently driving. This is because they are assessing your car's potential to be traded in, and they are trying to already weaken your position on one of the elements of the foursquare (which will be mentioned in a later chapter). If you do want to trade in your vehicle at the dealership, do not tell the salesperson that you're planning to trade in your car at this point. It might be even safer to say that you do not have a car. Tell the salesperson that you do not own a car or tell the salesperson that you currently take the bus. But, if you know you want to sell your car privately, telling the dealership that you would consider trading in your car in to them and allowing them to pay you significantly less than what your trade in is worth would allow the salesperson to feel more comfortable offering you a lower purchase price on your next car.

After this, the salesperson will help you decide what car you should drive next, based on your needs. After figuring out what kind of car you would like, the salesperson will probably suggest and have you test drive one or more cars. If you know what car you really want to get, and the salesperson has the car on the lot, he'll pull it out for you to test drive. Dealerships will also ask you for some personal information such as a copy of your driver's license and probably your Social Security or Social Insurance Number. In Canada, it is actually illegal to ask for your Social Insurance Number under these circumstances. This is so they can do a credit check on you to see what financing you can be approved for while you're doing your test drives.

When you do a test drive, push all the buttons to make sure they work. If the car is supposed to allow you to sync your phone to it via Bluetooth, sync it and see if you like how it works. Also, if the car you're looking to purchase is supposed to be able to download stuff from your phone, make sure that it can. If it is very important to you that your car is a V6 or V8, pop the hood and count the cylinders. If it's important that your vehicle goes into four-wheel-drive, find the button that transfers the car into four-wheel-drive. I have a story later on about one of my friends who thought she bought a four-wheel-drive car, but it turned out that she only bought a two-wheel-drive car, and she didn't find out until after she took the car home. Worse yet, she paid the dealership how much a four-wheel-drive version of the car would've cost. Also, when you test drive the car I would suggest driving it all around the city, highway (try passing people with it - but don't break any laws), on gravel, and over speed bumps. Make sure you know everything about it.

Also, look for signs of damage like the door being slightly off or a panel being repainted. These may be signs the car was previously in an accident. Get an independent vehicle accident report and make sure that you know the history. If it was indeed

Dealership Deceit

in an accident at one point, that doesn't mean you shouldn't purchase the vehicle (get an independent inspection from a mechanic before the purchase for sure) but it will strengthen your negotiating position. Also, just because the report says the vehicle was never in a collision does not mean that the vehicle was never in fact in a collision.

The awkward conversation about purchase price

After the test drive the salesperson will likely directly you to his office. At this point he may offer to get you a coffee, a coke or possibly offer you something to eat. This is to make you feel comfortable. After this happens, the salesperson will pull out a form and have you start filling it in. This is the form you will you and the dealership will use to negotiate how much you will pay for your car. You or the salesperson will fill in the estimated trade-in value of your car, the purchase price of the car you are looking to purchase, the amount you are willing to put down, and the monthly payment you're willing to pay. Even if you tell the salesperson you're selling your current car and financing the purchase of this car on your own, the salesperson will very likely still ask you to fill in how much you think the dealership should pay for your car, and how much you would like to pay per month. Filling these numbers in may not be a bad thing to do as it allows the salesperson and dealership manager to feel more comfortable offering you a low price for your purchase if they can overcharge you on financing and underpay you for your trade-in. This form will end up making several trips back and forth to the dealership manager's office where the dealership manager will fill in different numbers, bring it back to you, you fill in numbers, etc.. This form is called a foursquare. The next chapter will be devoted entirely to this form. If you are not careful, the dealership will deceive you into thinking you are getting a great deal but in reality the dealership ends up making a fortune from your purchase.

Takeaways

- Salespeople are not only aggressive because they want as many people as possible to buy cars from them, they're also scared of their managers. Managers have been known to fire a salesperson for letting customers just browse and leave their lot.

- Salespeople typically make from $60,000 a year or $100,000 a year, or even higher if they're really good at what they do.

- If you want to trade your car in to the dealership, don't tell the salesperson that you want to trade your car in and don't let the dealership know what you're driving. You'll weaken your position at the negotiating table. Approach the dealership in someone else's car, or take the bus.

- If you know you want to sell your car privately, it's okay to approach the dealership in your car. Letting the dealership think you are trading in your car to them may net you a lower purchase price.

**Be sure to check out the free bonuses at
www.dealershipdeceit.com!**

Summary

You should now have some insight into the true nature of the salespeople at the dealership. They are just people trying to do their job; however, the livelihood of their careers is dependent on whether or not you buy a car from them. Salespeople also have extra motivation from their manager to be as aggressive as possible trying to sell you a car. The next chapter will go into detail about the form salespeople and managers use to negotiate

Dealership Deceit

a purchase price with you. This form is very dangerous as salespeople and managers know how to use it to get you to overpay for your car yet make you think you got a great deal.

Chapter 5
The Foursquare of Deception

What is the foursquare ?

You may or may not have heard of the foursquare before. The foursquare is a very common form that dealerships use to negotiate the purchase price of a car with a potential buyer. Shown below is a diagram of the traditional foursquare.

CRAZY LARRY'S USED CARS
1234 Anywhere St.
Screwdover, MA 03311

MAKE/MODEL:
VIN:

I WILL BUY TODAY IF NUMBERS ARE
AGREEABLE TO THE PARTIES:

WORKSHEET

YOUR TRADE VALUE	PRICE
DOWN PAYMENT	MONTHLY PAYMENT

Credit: car buyerist.com

The form you use at your dealership may not look like this at all, but you will see the same headings somewhere on the form you will use; just not laid out as above.

We'll get into the negotiation aspect of the foursquare in a bit, but if you plan to lease your car, don't let the salesperson know right away. First get to a purchase price and a trade in value that you are okay with. The dealership and salesperson make less money on leases than they do all on full-out sales. Leasing complicates the foursquare a bit, so to make it easier we will first discuss how the foursquare works, then in the next chapter we'll add the lease components into the equation. Even if you know you're going to do a full purchase, I suggest you read the leasing chapter because it will contain some information that you may find interesting.

Okay, now onto the boxes in the foursquare.

Trade-in

In Chapter 2, it was mentioned that you should sell your car independently before approaching the dealership, or have plans to sell your car independently and not trade it in to the dealership. This is because the dealership will likely give you a lot less that you can get privately and will give you a lot less than what your car is actually worth. If you really want to trade in your car at a dealership, this section will explain to you how you can get the most from your trade-in.

Purchase Price

Next is the purchase price. If you're buying a new car, there will be a sticker price on the car. The dealership might put the dealer invoice price and the manufacturer suggested retail price (MSRP) on the car. They may also put a price next to that stating how much they want you to pay. The dealership does this because they know that probably 5 to 10% of potential customers will actually pay this higher amount. This means more profit for the dealership. Also, the dealership likes to add on special extras like rustproofing or paint protection to their cars on the lot. You can ask the dealership to remove these items from the purchase price, especially if you did not originally intend for your next car to have these extras. In the case of a used car, the original asking price of the car will likely be written on the car itself. You will be able to look up the wholesale value of your car on dealershipdeceit.com

You may also notice that the salesperson may write the purchase price on the foursquare using extremely large characters. This is one way for the salesperson or the dealership to establish that they're in the dominant position in the negotiation.

Down Payment

This is how much the dealership wants you to pay in cash today. It is true that the bank may need you to put a certain amount down; however, it is more likely that the dealership wants you to give them as much upfront profit as possible. But, it might be a good idea to put down as much is possible because this will mean lower monthly payments, and you will end up spending less on interest. Hopefully you have financing already sorted out before entering the dealership, so you should know how much money you will need to put down.

Monthly Payment

Here is where the dealership makes the most money! This box is also the reason you need to have your financing arranged before you visit the dealership. When people look to buy a car, and determine how much they want to pay, they don't look at the total purchase price; they look at how much monthly payment they can afford. They will work out their budget and decide they can afford maybe $250, $300, or even $350. This box makes the dealership a ton of money because after a customer tells the salesperson what they can afford for a monthly payment, the salesperson will ask the question "up to"? Almost every time, the customer will give a price $50 higher than the amount he or she stated before. The salesperson will then try to sell a car to the customer for the price of the number $50 higher than their original budget number. An extra $50 a month will net the dealership an extra $3,000 over five years. This is pure profit for the dealership and for the salesperson. Even if the salesperson can increase your monthly payments by $10, the salesperson will have increased in the dealership's profit by $600 over the span of five years. Dealerships will almost always sneak a couple extra dollars into the monthly payment. They know that most customers will not verify the monthly payment. They know that most customers will not calculate what monthly payment they should be making based on how much they're financing and the interest rate the dealership is offering them.

So, remember, if you are financing at the dealership and they give you a monthly payment, make sure that you confirm that the interest rate corresponds to that monthly payment. Download an app for your phone where you can punch in the interest rate and the amount you need to finance (the cost of the car minus your down payment minus the amount the dealership will pay you for your trade-in) and make sure that your app gives you the same monthly payment as the salesperson. Most free apps work just fine, but I've included a link to some free interest rate calculators at www.dealershipdeceit.com.

Dealership Deceit

When you start bidding on how much you want to pay, the salesperson will help you, or you will tell the salesperson what to put in each of the boxes. The salesperson may or may not provide input into the values that you suggest in each of the boxes. When you and salesperson feel comfortable about the numbers in each of the boxes, the salesperson will then bring this form to the dealership manager in the tower. Likely you will have to wait in the salesperson's office for a while before he or she comes back. Get comfortable, this may take a while. This is psychological manipulation where the salesperson (or in reality the dealership manager) wants you to feel impatient and anxious so they will have the upper hand in the negotiation. You bid numbers in your favor and you're anxiously hoping that the dealership will accept them. When the salesperson returns with from the dealership manager's office, she will show you the form with your numbers crossed out and replaced by new numbers presumably by the dealership manager. This is called the first pencil, and these numbers will likely shock you! Guess what? They are supposed to shock you. You are supposed to feel shocked and insulted! This is intentional. This opens the door for the salesperson to play good cop and for the dealership manager to play bad cop.

The salesperson will likely apologize and make an excuse for the horrifying numbers the manager replaced your numbers with.

After you proceed to storm out, and after she calms you and sits you back down, she may say that she just remembered that a rebate is available. Or she may say that her manager forgot about a promotion that might lower the payment amount or raise your trade-in value. You should know what the manufacturers rebates and promotions are, so don't let manufacturers rebates and incentives allow the dealership to justify a higher price. After you calmed down a bit, you will

Dan Christian

likely bid again against the dealership manager's numbers. The salesperson will cross out the dealership manager's numbers, and write down your numbers, and bring the form back to the tower.

The process where the salesperson fills in this foursquare is very interesting in of itself. He might ask you which numbers you have a problem with. You might say "all of them!" He may try again to have you decide what number bothers you the most. You might for instance say that you can only put down $2,000 when the first pencil came back with $4,000 for a down payment. The salesperson may confirm with you that you can only put $2,000 down, and he may very well write this $2,000 value in this particular box, crossing out the $4,000 amount written by the dealership manager. He may even ask you if you can commit to buying the car today if the dealership can make the numbers work with you only putting down $2,000. If you say yes, he might make you sign the bottom of the form to this effect. This signature is not legally binding in any way, but most people do not know this. He may then play around with the other numbers, i.e. decrease your trade-in credit by $1,000 and increase your total purchase price by $1,000. At this point he may fold over the sheet of paper hiding the trade-in value and the purchase so that you only see the down payment and purchase price amounts! And you may very well agree to these numbers, even if the dealership undervalues your trade-in and raises the purchase price higher than you would want it to be. But, you don't know this because these two boxes are hidden. You only see the down payment and monthly payment numbers, and even though these numbers may be a little higher than you were looking to pay, you will likely agree to the terms in the foursquare.

Something that you may want to consider doing: take a photo of the whole foursquare right before the salesperson brings it to the dealership manager. Also, take a photo of the foursquare with your phone after you sign the bottom of the form agreeing to the terms and the prices shown. Sometimes these foursquares disappear, and the negotiation will have to start all over again, and the terms may not be as much in your favor at the end of the re-negotiation as they were before.

After making you wait again, the salesperson will bring a second pencil with all the numbers crossed out again and replaced with insulting numbers, although not as insulting as before. You may end up counter offering and sending the form back to the dealership manager, but at some point the dealership manager will come out of the tower and speak with you directly. Or, you may be directed into the tower. At this point, the dealership manager might be willing to give you something pretty close to what you originally wanted, but he might want you to sign at the bottom of the page saying that if you agree to these numbers that you will buy the car today (if you haven't done so before), and only if you leave a deposit with the dealership. This is psychological manipulation. Just because you sign the bottom of this form saying that what the price will be if you're to buy the car today does not actually mean that you need to buy the car today. Also, there is a very good chance that the deposit that you would leave with the dealership is refundable (of course confirm this before handing over any money).

Remember when I said that an average car salesperson sells about 15 to 20 cars per month, and that you buy a car once every 3 to 7 years? And those salespeople are way more experienced at selling cars than you are at buying cars? Here's where it shows. The salesperson is very proficient at executing this foursquare to perfection, to confuse you and to play with your emotions. Eventually, there might be a time where you just get very frustrated and as long as you get the monthly payment that you want and get to put down the down payment that you were hoping to pay, you'll sign whatever you need to sign to get the car.

Oh, and another thing. If at some point during the negotiation process either the salesperson or the dealership manager offers you something, make sure it's written down on that foursquare! To get you to agree to a higher purchase price, or to get you to agree to a price above the MSRP, they may offer you an accessory package or a moon roof at no extra charge. In the case of GM, they may offer you an OnStar integrated rear-view mirror. An Acura dealership might offer you Acuralink at no charge. There are cases where these items will be offered at the negotiation process but magically forgotten about in the finance and insurance office.

Here's what a completed foursquare will look like:

Credit: car buyerist.com

Dealership Deceit

Does it look confusing? That's the idea. This form and way it's filled out is designed to make you feel uncomfortable, thereby making it easier for the salesperson and the dealership manager to make you accept a higher price or motivate you to accept a lower value for your trade-in.

Takeaways

- Download an app for your phone where you can punch in the interest rate and the amount you need to finance (purchase price of the car minus your down payment minus the amount the dealership will credit you for your trade-in) and make sure your app gives you the same monthly payment as the salesperson.

- The foursquare is designed to confuse you. Salespeople and dealership managers will expertly move from square to square in an effort to confuse you. Focus as much as you can on only the purchase price. If the salesperson or the dealership manager folds this sheet or turns it over, make sure that you look at the entire form before agreeing to the numbers.

- If the salesperson offers you a special incentive to have you agree to buy a car with him, make sure it's written down! If the salesperson offers you free window tinting or free 3M coatings, make sure that it says so on the foursquare.

- Take a photo of the foursquare with your smart phone so if any changes are made later you have proof of what was agreed to.

- Make sure that you understand what incentives the manufacturer is offering new car buyers, and make sure that

Dan Christian

the dealership is not offering these incentives on their behalf to justify making you pay a higher price. You are entitled to any incentives offered by the manufacturer, whether or not the dealership uses them in the negotiation to justify a higher purchase price.

Be sure to check out the free bonuses at
www.dealershipdeceit.com!

Okay, we made it through the negotiation process. If you've done everything in Chapter 2, you should have a good purchase price negotiated with the dealership. If you are trading in your current vehicle, and you plan to finance with the dealership, hopefully you have a pretty good trade-in value and a good monthly payment hammered out. The next chapter deals with how leasing fits into the foursquare equation and negotiation. If you are 100% sure you will not lease through the dealership, you can skip the next chapter. Chapter 7 will discuss what happens next in the process; you will be directed to the finance and insurance office where you will meet with another salesperson (even though you won't think he's a salesperson at first). However, I still suggest that you read the next chapter because it is good information for you know and you may consider leasing in the future.

Chapter 6
Leasing

Hopefully at this point you have a good grasp on how the foursquare works. You should understand what each of the boxes mean, and how the dealership can deceive you into paying more for your car while making you think you're getting a great deal. Now, if you're planning to lease your next vehicle, there are some additional factors that you need to consider. Firstly, I would suggest not telling the salesperson right away that you are looking to lease. Dealerships make less money on a lease than they do on a sale, so they will be less open to selling you a car for less if they know that you intend to lease rather than buy.

I mentioned earlier in this book that if you want to purchase a luxury car or a fancy sports car, from a financial point of view you should consider leasing it rather than purchasing it. Cars are a depreciating asset, and you should be renting depreciating assets rather than purchasing and owning them. Leasing is very beneficial if you cannot otherwise afford a higher-end car, or you wish to pay less on a monthly basis for your high-end car, and you plan to trade it in for a newer car after a few years. Also, leasing should require little to no down payment. If your dealership requires you to put down a substantial down payment, consider doing business with another dealership.

As mentioned earlier, when you lease a car from a dealership, you essentially rent it. When you rent the car from a dealership, you pay a monthly rental fee. This monthly rental fee is comprised of depreciation plus an interest rate (profit for the dealership), and other fees and taxes.

The lease negotiation is very similar to the foursquare negotiation. There is still a trade-in box, a purchase price spot, a monthly payment box, and a down payment box. Just like with the purchase, you'll want to negotiate the purchase price of the vehicle to be as low as possible, and you'll want the purchase price to govern your negotiation. Also, just like with the purchase, you will want to sell your vehicle privately if you're planning to do a trade-in. You should know coming into the negotiation what the MSRP is and what the dealer invoice price is.

Where the lease negotiation differs from a purchase negotiation is that instead of negotiating an interest rate, the interest rate is actually pre-set by the manufacturer and the lending institution. This interest rate is called a money factor. Money factors are not negotiable. You may be able to find a bank that may offer a lower money factor for you if you shop around. Another term that is used in leasing but not in purchasing is residual value. The residual value of a car is the market value of the car at the end of the lease period. You will have the option at the end of the lease period to purchase your car for the residual price. I'll tell you later why this is not a good idea.

To calculate the monthly payment (you can also find a spreadsheet at www.dealershipdeceit.com which will do this math for you), you will need to subtract the residual price of the car from the negotiated price of the car. You will then need to divide this by the amount of months in your lease term. Most leases are for 36 months. It is inadvisable to have a lease longer than 36 months. After you do this calculation you'll come up with a monthly depreciation amount. Next, to calculate the interest payment, you will need to add the depreciation amount

Dealership Deceit

to the agreed purchase price and multiply this by the money factor. After you do this, you will have a monthly interest rate or monthly money factor. Next you need to add these two numbers together, and add any fees or taxes that your state or province might have. This should be your monthly payment. Remember to confirm this number on your own before agreeing to the numbers on the foursquare. Sometimes dealerships like to charge a higher interest rate differential than set out by the manufacturer. This results in a little bit of extra profit for the dealership without you knowing it.

Something else to keep in mind is that you'll want to purchase at the times mentioned in the Timing section on page 7. In the case of leasing, you will want to avoid initiating a lease agreement right before next year's models are released. Initiating a lease agreement right before next year's models are released may net a lower residual value as the model that you're looking to lease will essentially be a year old right when next year's models are released. Remember, you want the difference between the agreed-upon purchase price and the residual value be as low as possible to ensure you have the lowest monthly payment possible.

Also, the value of a used car (as soon as you drive your new lease off the lot, it becomes classified as a used car) partially depends on the mileage of the car. You will need to determine how many miles or kilometers you are allowed to drive the vehicle over the term of the lease, and you will need to know the penalty per mile or kilometer if you exceed this amount. Figure out how many miles or kilometers you anticipate driving and leave yourself some wiggle room just in case you may go over. If you go on an extended road trip, you may need to consider renting another vehicle so you avoid paying mileage charges.

Lastly, you will be given the option to purchase the car at the residual price at the end of your lease. I highly recommend against doing this (although you are more than welcome to) because there is a very good chance that as this car is now essentially three years old, you'll be able to find it and negotiate at this or another dealership as a used car for a much better price than the residual price listed on the lease agreement. Although you have very little say as to what you would like the residual price to be, you want the residual price to be as high as possible to reduce your monthly lease payments, but you want your monthly payments or total payment for your car purchase to be as low as possible.

Takeaways

- Make sure you know the rebates and incentives offered by the manufacturer; don't let the dealership offer these as justification for a higher price.

- Do the math yourself and make sure that the dealership is using the right money factor and not skimming profit off the top.

**Be sure to check out the free bonuses at
www.dealershipdeceit.com!**

Okay, hopefully you have some insight into how leases work and how to reduce your monthly payments and pay as little as possible for your lease. Also, hopefully you understand some of the extra terminology that is used in a lease negotiation, which is not normally used when you purchase a vehicle. In the next chapter, I'll explain how you can get dealerships to voluntarily offer you the lowest price possible for the car you're looking to buy or lease. Sound exciting? Then keep reading!

Chapter 7
The 2-Dealership Method™

As mentioned in the previous chapters, the dealership will make you go through the foursquare process to come up with the monthly payments, down payment, trade-in value, and purchase price that both you and the dealership agree to. Also, as mentioned in previous chapters, salespeople and managers at dealerships are far more experienced at negotiating the purchase price of a car than you are. There is no question that salespeople at dealerships have the upper hand at the negotiating table. However, there is a way for you to gain back some of the negotiating power. I call this the 2-Dealership Method™. The 2-Dealership Method™ involves you having two salespeople and two managers at two different dealerships negotiating against each other for your business, rather than you negotiating by yourself against one dealership.

The 2-Dealership Method™ involves you leaving the dealership after completing the foursquare process, and signing the bottom of the form saying that you will buy the car today. You then come up with an excuse to leave the dealership, i.e. you have to pick up your kids from school or you have a doctor's appointment etc. The dealership thinks you intend to buy the car because you signed on the bottom of the form saying you will buy today, and you left a deposit. When you leave the dealership, you actually head over to another dealership. It's best if this dealership is not owned by the same person who owns the first dealership. If you've completed all the steps in Chapter 2, you already know which dealership to go to. If you don't, just head to another dealership offering the same car or

57

the same brand of car. You then proceed to tell them what deal you have reached with the first dealership and ask if they can do better. Due to the nature of dealerships, salespeople, and managers, of course they can do better than the first dealership! They will likely have you test drive the exact same version of the car you have under contract with the first dealership, or a very similar car. They will then put you through the foursquare process, although this process will likely be much easier for you than the foursquare process at the first dealership. You will then proceed to sign the bottom of the paper saying you will buy the car today, and if you haven't already done so leave a deposit. After this is done, you ask them if you can go back to the first dealership to get your money back because you want to do business with the second dealership.

When you head back to the first dealership to get your money back, guess what will happen? They will likely ask you why you want to get your deposit back. You will tell them that you have actually gone to a second dealership and they were able to offer you a better price. In my experience, dealerships do not easily return your deposit. They will likely try to find out what numbers the second dealership offered you, and they will proceed to offer you something better! After you agree to this better offer, you tell the first dealership that you want to go to the second dealership and get your deposit back. At some point the dealership made threaten to not give your deposit back to you. One recourse you have is threatening to go to the regulatory body that I mentioned you need to look up in Chapter 2. I also have a story about how I bought my most recent car at the time of writing this book, where I used the 2-Dealership Method™ without realizing it, at www.dealershipdeceit.com.

As already mentioned, it's important to make sure that the two dealerships are not owned by the same person or company.

Dealership Deceit

Also, unfortunately the best dealerships for you to have negotiate against each other may not be in your home town; when I bought my most recent car I had to drive to a dealership 2.5 hours away.

Variation

I personally have had success visiting two different dealerships and having the salespeople negotiate against each other. A variation on this technique that my colleagues have used successfully is to do the foursquare process with more than one dealership via email. They'll email one dealership and ask them what the best price is that they can give them. Then they'll email another dealership which has the same car in stock and ask if they can beat the price given to them by the first dealership. They do this until they reach a point where the prices don't go down. Of course you still need to test drive the car and make sure they don't do a "bait and switch". A bait and switch is where customers are "baited" by a dealership advertising a very reasonable sale price on a car they're selling, but when customers visit the dealership, they discover that the car is in fact not available, giving the salespeople the opportunity to pressure the customer into purchasing a similar, but higher priced car ("switching"). Also, they will still get you to buy all the extended warranties and add-ons in the finance and insurance office (discussed in the next chapter).

Of course, don't be a jerk about this. The salesperson and the dealership managers will not appreciate that you're grinding them for a lower price resulting in less profit for the salesperson and for the dealership. Be a hard and decisive negotiator, but understand these guys are working harder for your business than a typical salesperson or manager will work, and they are earning less profit from you than from a typical car buyer.

Takeaways

- You don't need to leave the first dealership only right after you have completed the foursquare and signed the bottom of the sheet. You can also leave any time during the finance and insurance process (explained later), before you pay the remainder of your down payment, sign the bottom of the purchase agreement, receive your keys, and the dealership receives the keys to your trade-in.

- If the dealership tells you that your refundable deposit is actually not refundable, they're very likely wrong about this. Remember that step in Chapter 2 where I ask you to find out who the regulating body is in your state or province? Threaten to go to this body if the dealership refuses to give you your deposit back.

- Ensure that the two dealerships are not owned by the same person or company.

**Be sure to check out the free bonuses at
www.dealershipdeceit.com!**

Summary

At this point you should have negotiated a very good price with good terms at the dealership of your choice using the 2-Dealership Method™. After this negotiation, you will be led into a finance and insurance office to meet with a finance manager to sign some final paperwork and get your keys. But, is the negotiation and deception really over? Read on to find out.

Chapter 8
Finance and Insurance

Whew, the hard part is over, now I just have to sign the papers (oops)

Okay, you just have gotten the deal of a lifetime! You've gotten a lot of extras, you've gotten a very low purchase price, and if you're financing at the dealership, you got an excellent rate! The negotiation is over, right? The only thing that's left is just to sign some paperwork and get your keys, right? Well, you can probably guess the answer to this question.

After this foursquare is signed, you'll be directed to a finance and insurance office. You'll be talking with a finance manager, but please note that this person is a salesperson as well. You just do not know it yet. Believe it or not, especially in the case of new car sales, dealerships make more money in this office than they do on the showroom floor.

According to the National Automobile Dealers Association, an average dealership loses about $100 per new car sale. Car buyers are becoming more and more educated and learning how much they should actually be purchasing their car for. So, dealerships need to come up with more creative ways of making a profit from selling cars.

At this point, the finance and insurance manager will probably show you a menu of extended warranties and other goodies that you should buy. They'll likely explain how each one is beneficial for you. They will explain the merits of, and what is included

61

in, each extended warranty. If you feel you need an extended warranty for your vehicle, please feel free to purchase one, but please keep in mind that it's highly unlikely you will need it.

When you buy an extended warranty, you're making a bet that your car is going to need repairs that are worth more than the amount you paid for your warranty. The dealership is also making a bet. They're betting that your car is not going to require repairs that will cost more than they are charging you for the extended warranty. Who do you think is more likely to win the bet? Dealerships make a lot of money on extended warranties, and most of the time these extended warranties are not required.

Most if not all new cars come with manufacturer's warranties, and if you're looking for a used car, the manufacturer's warranty may still be applicable. Also, most dealerships (at least reputable dealerships) will not sell cars that will break down soon after they leave the lot. The maintenance will likely be up to date. If you are concerned, bring it to a third body automotive inspection facility. If you're buying a certified used vehicle, it should already be coming with a warranty. Extended warranties should not be required. It is actually more beneficial for you to save the amount that you would have originally put into an extended warranty on the side and keep that money for yourself, or to fix the car yourself if needed.

When I bought my first car at a dealership, I originally declined the extended warranty. The car was still under the manufacturer's warranty, but after I declined the extended warranty, the finance manager asked me if I was a poker player. I was confused. The finance manager said that I'm gambling with my car. "You're a gambler. You must be really good poker player if you're going to decline the extended warranty on a used car." I fell for his trick and I ended up buying a warranty

Dealership Deceit

that I did not need. The car that I bought did not need to be serviced until a few years after the extended warranty period expired.

After you're done with the extended warranties, the finance person will likely proceed on to other options that you will have the ability to purchase. These options may include undercoating, cloth protectant, leather guard protectant, paint protectant, window etching, all weather mats, etc., and are just another way for dealerships to make a profit. If you're purchasing or leasing a new car, this along with an extended warranty may be the only way dealership can turn a profit from the sale. Paint protectant is more often than not just very fancy and overpriced polish. The amount of money that dealerships charge to protect your leather or etch your windows is outrageous compared to what you would pay if you were to get it done at a body shop afterwards. 99% of these extra options are not needed. However, the finance manager has ways of convincing you that you need something. For example, they might say you need paint protectant, and then the finance manager may show you a video of a car lit on fire, burning up or exploding on their phone. They'll tell you that the car does not have their paint protectant. Then they'll show you another car that is lit on fire but doesn't explode, and will tell you it was because of the paint protectant.

As long as you regularly maintain your leather on your own, and you moisturize and condition it regularly according to the owners' manual, you do not need the leather guard offered by the dealership. All-weather mats can be bought at an auto supply store for much less than the dealership will sell them for. Another thing the finance manager might say is that your car has more computer chips in it than the space shuttle. While this may be true depending on which car you're purchasing, this is just another way for the dealership to scare you into buying an extended warranty.

63

If the salesperson agreed to give you something for free, i.e. 3M coating, winter tires, or all-weather mats, make sure it shows up on the purchase agreement that you will be getting these items at no cost to you.

If you need to, practice saying no. Practice having a friend offering you weird things that you can buy at any automotive store, and practice saying no. This might sound silly, but it will be much harder to say no when the finance manager is offer you compelling reasons why you need to buy dealership extras.

The only item I would suggest you consider getting, if it makes sense, is the tire warranty. The tire warranty might only cost you $200 or $250, but if you live in a city where there are a lot of potholes, you will likely bend a rim or puncture your tire within the warranty period, and this warranty may pay for itself.

One other extra which is worth getting (but not through the dealership) is gap insurance. Gap insurance covers the difference between the amount owing on your loan and the actual value of the car. As discussed on several occasions, the value of your car dramatically decreases the moment you drive it off the lot. However, the amount owing on a loan steadily decreases over time. Unless you're buying your car in cash, you will almost have more owing on your loan than the value of your car throughout the first few years. In the event that you lose your car in an accident, the insurance adjuster may only pay out the value of your car at the time. This amount will not be enough to cover the balance of your loan. Gap insurance covers the remainder of the balance. But don't get this through the dealership. You can likely get gap insurance through your regular vehicle insurance provider.

Lastly, you might also want to go through your financing documents if you financed the car at the dealership. Make sure

Dealership Deceit

that these documents are actually from a bank and that you're actually approved for credit. Sometimes dealerships just give you an estimate of what they think you can be approved for based on the credit score they give you. You need to be wary of what's called a spot delivery scam. Dealerships may run the scam with potential buyers with less than ideal credit.

To ensure that you do not fall prey to the spot delivery scam, make sure that you have purchase documents, registration, insurance, and a new plate right when you leave the dealership, or soon after. You own the car if you have signed papers, regardless of whether or not the car is financed. Your credit must have been good or the dealer would not have delivered the car to you at the price that you agreed to pay. Finance documentation showing payments, deposit, interest rate, and other financial items is a legally binding contract. This gives you specific legal rights. You own a car only subject to making payments. That cannot be changed by the dealership or anyone else wanting to take possession.

I suggest that you keep all your paperwork and anything else associated with the sale. This includes any calendars, photographs, advertising etc. If the finance manager asks you for papers any time after the purchase, refuse to do this. Make sure that you keep all this documentation somewhere safe, but do not keep it in the car. Lastly, if you're asked to come back to dealership to sign some additional papers, make sure you do not come back with the car you bought. Come back in a friend's car, or take the bus. Also have a family member or friend witness what is being told to you. If a dispute arises with the dealer about the contract, and the dealer demands the car is returned, park it in a garage or a remote location until the matter is resolved to prevent it from being taken against you will. Put together a complete timeline of everything that happened from the time you thought that you purchased the car until the car was taken away. Do your best to remember the names of the people in the dealership and any statements ever made to you during conversations with salespeople, dealership managers, and finance managers. Keep track of all the money you had invested into the purchase, registration, insurance, down payments, and how much you were credited with your trade-in. If you do pay cash, always get a receipt.

Also, make sure you know what the return policy is, if there is any. Especially if it's a new car you likely won't be able to return it, but it would be nice to know what your options are.

Okay, so you are ready to sign the final purchase agreement, pay the rest of your down payment, and receive your keys! Go through this document very carefully. Go through it line by line, word for word, and make sure everything makes sense to you. If you bought a car that has four-wheel-drive, make sure it says four-wheel-drive in the purchase agreement. If you bought a car with a diesel engine, an in-dash navigation system, Eco boost, or Acuralink, make sure this is all mentioned in the purchase agreement. If you are looking to buy a V6 or a V8, make sure the purchase agreement says V6 or V8.

A couple of years ago my friend was purchasing a SUV. She wanted an all-wheel-drive vehicle, and she told the salesperson that she wanted an all-wheel-drive vehicle. She took it for a test drive, but she never bothered to look for the button that switched the vehicle to all-wheel-drive. She asked the dealership manager to confirm that the vehicle did indeed have all-wheel-drive capabilities. The dealership manager verbally confirmed to her that yes the vehicle was in fact an all-wheel-drive vehicle. She signed the paperwork and took her vehicle home. At home, out of curiosity, she tried putting her vehicle into all-wheel-drive. She wasn't able to find the button to do so, and she started to get worried that maybe her vehicle was not capable of all-

Dealership Deceit

wheel-drive at all. She tried going back to the dealership and complaining, but she had a purchase agreement in her hands which said that she agreed to purchase a two-wheel-drive vehicle. Worse yet, the price she agreed to was the MSRP of the all-wheel-drive version of her vehicle.

Moral of the story? If there is something unique about the vehicle that is important to you, make sure it says that it's included on the purchase agreement! And make sure it's in the physical car! By this time you'll have been negotiating for a couple solid days with different dealerships. You'll be tired. Dealerships will count on you to miss something because of your weakened state of mind. Make sure, make sure, and make sure that the final purchase price at the end of document is as close as possible to that purchase price the salesperson and you agreed to at the end of the foursquare. There are fees that you will not be able to get out of paying, such as state or provincial registration fees. If there are fees on there that you do not want, ask the person to cross it out. The finance and insurance manager will likely tell you can or cannot cross out something, but they will make you feel guilty for crossing it out. Cross it out anyway.

If you're purchasing a new car, you might be assessed delivery fees. Unfortunately, it is very unlikely you will be able to get out of paying this fee. This fee covers the cost of delivering the car from the manufacturer to the dealership that you're at, and this fee is levied by the manufacturer. This fee is unique to the car buying world because buyers are not usually subject to delivery charges. If you buy ice cream from an ice cream stand, you do not need to pay for the ice cream to be shipped from the factory to the stand. When you buy coffee from a coffee shop, you do not need to pay to have the coffee beans shipped from the processing plant to the coffee shop. As a car buyer, you will need to ensure that you do not get double charged on delivery charges.

If you're leasing a car, make sure you are signing a lease agreement. Make sure that the residual value, the money factor, and the monthly depreciation payments are correct. Make sure you're also clear about how many miles or kilometers you can drive your car, and what the penalty is if you go beyond your mileage. Make sure you're also clear about the condition of your vehicle upon return.

The dealership will also likely charge you a documentation fee or processing fee. Try to get this fee removed. If the dealership is very reluctant to do this, you likely got a good deal on your purchase. If the dealership waives this fee with no objections, it might be a red flag that you're paying more for the car than you could be. Remember, even now you can still walk out!

Once you sign the purchase agreement, you will get a copy and you will receive the keys to the car you are purchasing (and the dealership will receive the keys to your trade-in). You have now legally and officially bought the car. Congratulations!

Takeaways

- Keep your eyes on the final purchase price. Dealerships always try to include extra things into the purchase agreement which you may or may not have verbally agreed to.

- If you're financing at the dealership, verify the monthly payment for yourself; punch the amount you need to finance for on an app on your smartphone, punch in the interest rate, and make sure the monthly payment is correct.

- Make sure your down payment includes the deposit if financing with the dealership.

Dealership Deceit

- Decline as much as you can. When the dealership tries to sell you an extended warranty, they are betting that your car will not break down so they can make a profit on your warranty purchase. If anything, you should be worried if they do not try selling you an extended warranty.

- If there's anything offered to you in this office that entices you, get it done outside the dealership. The dealership will sell the service to you at twice or three times the cost it would be for you to get it done at a body shop.

- If you and the salesperson agreed to have something thrown in for free, make sure it shows up on the purchase agreement.

- If you're buying a car that is an all-wheel-drive, make sure that the contract said that your car has all-wheel-drive. If you're looking to buy a V6 or V8 car, make sure that the contract says V6 or V8 (and make sure you physically looked at the car and counted the cylinders).

- Get gap insurance (with your insurance broker, not the dealership).

Be sure to check out the free bonuses at
www.dealershipdeceit.com!

Congratulations! You just bought (or leased) yourself a car, and hopefully you got some really great terms and a really great price. The next chapter talks a little bit about no-haggle dealerships. Because car buyers are becoming more and more aware about what the dealer invoice price or the wholesale price of their vehicles are, and because dealerships know that car buyers do not like haggling at a dealership, more and more dealerships are becoming no-haggle dealerships.

Chapter 9
No-Haggle Dealerships

With the Internet becoming more and more mainstream, car buyers have the ability to look up the wholesale price and the dealer invoice price of vehicles that they want to potentially buy. With this, dealerships are starting to notice that they no longer have the upper hand when it comes to knowing how much the cars they are buying from and selling to their customers are actually worth. Also, dealerships are very much aware that most car buyers detest the negotiation and haggling process. In the past, they could have used the fact that car buyers do not like haggling with them to their advantage. They could have worn down the potential buyers and brainwashed them into believing that their trade-in and the car they are looking to purchase is what they say it is. With these two things in mind, dealerships are now starting to become no-haggle dealerships.

At a no-haggle dealership, car buyers pay the price for the car that is listed on the car. On the no-haggle dealership's website, the price listed is the price the car buyer will pay. If you completely detest the showroom haggling process, you will find no-haggle dealerships very appealing.

You will not have to worry about getting into a situation where you actually end up haggling at a no-haggle dealership. If a dealership brands themselves as a no-haggle dealership but they still haggle with their customers, their brand and reputation will be tarnished and they even may face penalties. If you choose to visit a no-haggle dealership, you can be rest assured that you will pay the sticker price or the price shown online or on print advertising for the car.

Cars listed for sale at a no-haggle dealership may be listed for a lot or a little over the wholesale price or the dealer invoice price. You will not be able to employ the 2-Dealership Method™ in order to get two no-haggle dealerships to negotiate against each other to give you the best price. All you can do is find out how much each of the various no-haggle dealerships are selling the car for, find out how much they will pay you for your trade-in, and how much your financing will be, and you will have to go with the dealership that gives you the best numbers.

The process for buying a car at a no-haggle dealership is similar to buying a car at a dealership that haggles. You will still enter the dealership, you will still be accosted by a salesperson who will attempt to find out what vehicle you're currently driving, and they will still help you decide what car you should buy. You will still go on a test drive while the dealership may or may not do a credit check on you, then you will be seated at the salesperson's office. She will still pull out a foursquare for you and her to fill in. However, the key difference is the purchase price of the car is non-negotiable. The price that is written down is the price that you will end up paying. Also, the value of your trade-in is not negotiable. The manager or salesperson will evaluate your trade-in and tell you how much they will pay for it. Also, your financing options at the dealership itself are rigid.

However, these dealerships still need to make money, even if they are selling the car for very close to dealer invoice and wholesale price. Guess how they do this? Along with notoriously undervaluing their customer's trade-in, they do this in the finance and insurance office. They will still try to sell you a list of warranties, upgrades, and options that you will likely not need, or will be overpriced and you can get for a much more

Dealership Deceit

reasonable price afterwards at any auto body place. So, will you save money buying at a no-haggle dealership? Well, it depends. If you do not have the stomach or the willingness (or the time) to haggle at a dealership, the no-haggle dealership is the way to go. However, if you play your cards right, you will likely be able to get a better purchase price or more value at a dealership where you can haggle. Don't forget that financing is also more expensive at a dealership than on your own, and no-haggle dealerships will very likely pay you even less for your trade-in than a haggle dealership. At a dealership that allows you to haggle, you can deceive them into thinking you will finance with them and that you will trade in your car to get a better purchase price, and then you can take your trade-in and financing off the table at the last second. At a no-haggle dealership, the purchase price is set in stone whether you finance with a trade-in to the dealership or you sell your car on your own and find your own financing.

Tesla is doing this – in a different way

Other dealerships are moving towards yet another model. Tesla is one such company. Most dealerships are franchises. They may specialize in a certain brand or represent a certain manufacturer, but they are most often owner operated franchises. Tesla has adopted a different model. While they do have showrooms all across North America, each showroom is owned by the manufacturer, not by an owner operator. Car buyers primarily buy Teslas online. To purchase or lease a Tesla, all a car buyer needs to do is go to the Tesla website, set up the purchase online, and have the Tesla delivered right to their door. There is no haggling, and all the profits from each new sale go directly to the manufacturer.

73

Takeaways

- No-haggle dealerships offer peace of mind for car buyers that absolutely detest haggling.

- Numbers are set in stone whether or not the buyer finances with the dealership or trades their car in to the dealership.

- The buying process is essentially the same outside of the foursquare process.

- No-haggle dealerships still hard sell you on warranties and add-ons in the finance and insurance office.

- They likely do not pose a financial advantage to dealerships that allow haggling.

Be sure to check out the free bonuses at www.dealershipdeceit.com!

Summary

In this chapter we discussed a bit about how no-haggle dealerships operate and how Tesla is starting to change how cars are sold. Remember, just because you're buying from a no-haggle dealership, that doesn't mean that the dealership won't try selling you overpriced extras. The last chapter of this book is an action plan for you! Armed with the knowledge from this book, you are now ready to purchase your next car! Please also visit www.dealershipdeceit.com for some exciting free bonuses for you to enjoy.

Chapter 10
Your Action Plan

Time for action! The following is an action plan that you can follow that incorporates most if not all the techniques discussed in this book. You can also find an updated and printable version of this action plan at www.dealershipdeceit.com. If all you do is follow this action plan and skip over reading the rest of this book, you will already save thousands on your next car purchase.

- Decide you want to buy a car.

    - Why do you want another car?

        - Is it because your circumstances changed i.e. you having a bigger family and you need a bigger vehicle or a 4 door vehicle?

        - Is it because your current car is old and falling apart and not worth the money to spend fixing it?

        - Is it because you just feel bored with your current car? (It's okay to feel this way.)

        - If this is the reason, why? What don't you like about your car anymore? Have you considered detailing the inside of your current car, tuning it up and having minor repairs done on it, or installing an updated stereo system or in-dash navigation? Doing this is likely much cheaper than purchasing another car and may help ease your feelings of boredom with your current car.

- Decide what car you want to get based on your needs.

- Decide if you want to purchase new or used, and if you want to purchase or lease.

  - If you want a new car, lease it. If you want a used car, purchase it. If you want a fancy car but can't afford one, rent it for a weekend once every couple of months. You don't need to drive it every day.

- Learn how long the warranty is on the car, learn what the warranty covers (bumper to bumper, powertrain only, technology only, etc.), and in the case of a new car learn what incentives the manufacturer is offering that month so the dealership doesn't offer those incentives to justify a higher price.

- Figure out how much you can afford for a down payment and a monthly payment (unless you want to buy full in cash).

- If you want to trade your car in at the dealership, don't, sell it privately.

- Get your financing sorted out on your own with a bank (don't tell the dealerships that you have your own financing until you have a price negotiated).

  - Know what interest rate you qualify for.

  - Know what your bank or broker needs for a down payment.

Dealership Deceit

- Find out who regulates dealerships in your state or province.

- Find dealerships that have the car you want online within your local area, narrow down to two, you may need to be willing to travel away from your home city.

  - Make sure they're both not owned by the same person or company.

  - Make sure they're not a no-haggle dealership if you intend to haggle for a lower price.

- Employ the 2-Dealership Method™. Call them to put deposits on the cars to make sure they're really at the dealerships and make appointments to see both.

  - They may even still bait you into the dealership to try selling you a more expensive car.

- Go to the first one, test drive the car, and negotiate a price. Sign the bottom of the form saying you agree to buy the car today.

  - Always ensure you have the keys to your car at all times until you have officially purchased your next car. Make sure you always have the ability to walk out.

- Make an excuse to leave but promise to come back later that day. They have a signed form and a deposit so they will be confident you will buy from them.

- Visit the next dealership and tell them what terms you have with the first dealership.

- Wanting your business, they will have you test drive their car and negotiate a better price with you. Sign the bottom of that form and leave a deposit. Tell them you will get the deposit back from the first dealership.

- Go back to the first dealership, tell them you agreed to buy the car at the second dealership because they offered you a better price, and ask for your deposit back.

- Go back and forth between the two until you have the price you want.

- When you have the price you want, confirm the numbers and terms.

  - Confirm that the monthly payment on the form is correct based on the interest rate the dealership is offering you i.e. calculate it yourself using an interest rate calculator app.

  - If you're leasing, confirm that they are using the correct money factor and residual values.

  - If something was offered to you as an incentive to justify a higher price, make sure it's written down on the form and take a photo of this form with your phone.

- Go into the finance and insurance office.

- Decline as much of the extended warranties and extra goodies as you can.

  - There's a very good chance you can get the goodies for much cheaper later on somewhere else.

Dealership Deceit

- Go through the final purchase agreement – make sure that the stuff that you absolutely need in your car (i.e. V8 or in-dash navigation or 4 wheel drive) is written on the purchase agreement AND you can find that stuff in the car.

- Ensure the purchase price is what you agreed to in the showroom when you sign the purchase agreement.

Made in the USA
San Bernardino, CA
18 October 2015